Swallowing My Mother

Swallowing My Mother

Catherine Moss

FRONTENAC HOUSE
Calgary

Cover and Book Design by EPIX Design Inc.

National Library of Canada Cataloguing in Publication Data

Moss, Catherine.
  Swallowing my mother

Poems.
ISBN 0-9684903-3-6

I. Title.
PS8576O7862S9 2001   C811'.6   C2001-910119-8
PR9199.3.M659S9 2001

Printed and Bound in Canada

Published by Frontenac House Ltd.
1138 Frontenac Avenue S.W.
Calgary, AB   T2T 1B6
Canada
Tel: (403) 245-2491 Fax: (403) 245-2380
E-mail: editor@frontenachouse.com
Website: www.frontenachouse.com

1 2 3 4 5 6 7 8 9   05 04 03 02 01

Acknowledgments

Some of these poems first appeared in Dandelion, Canadian Verse 2, Matrix, New Quarterly, Other Voices, Outposts (England), Prairie Fire, Prism International, The Antigonish Review, The Fiddlehead, The New Delta Review (United States), The Prairie Journal of Canadian Literature, Whetstone and Windsor Review.

The Canadian Broadcast Corporation has aired several selections of these poems on Alberta Anthology.

I am especially grateful to Su Croll,
Cecelia Frey, Carl Svoboda and Hector Williamson,
Richard Harrison, the Markin-Flanagan Writer-in-Residence at the University of Calgary, 1995-1996,
Yvonne Trainer,
Shirley Black and the 'Tuesday Morning Group',
The Alexandra Writers' Centre Society,
and the many friends, colleagues and instructors whose advice, support and encouragement have been invaluable.

My loving thanks to P.E.F. for his tolerance of the hours I spend in the computer's company.

Table of Contents

Swallowing My Mother

A Glossary of Green

Roving Doesn't Mean We'll Never Come Home

Swallowing My Mother

Self Portrait

this is you choosing a mother
by candlelight
you lick her voice slowly
like quince jelly from a silver
dessert spoon
you are dressed
in vermilion taffeta
perfectly needled
drawn straight over the curve of your breasts
your finger ringed
with gold and a ruby cluster
blackberry dark
the banquet is a still life
of bloomed grapes
William pears and Camembert melting
from the cut
in its tallow yellow heart
   look at your hand
the way the candle light
creates translucent flesh
the way you are gesturing
no

in this photograph of me   my mother
grandmother   sister
(my father   still absent
is behind the camera)
the sepia gestures are tiny
a clenched hand
a grip on a skirt

I lean against my mother
    my long legged older sister
has just been shouted down from the chestnut tree
and stands apart
anticipating
fracture
the kidnapping of my mother
by a man who lives in Africa

we fear my mother
is the willing hostage
of my father
a hunter who claims antelope
welcome his bullet
he has already captured her eyes
    in a fiftieth of a second
she will rip
my hand from her skirt
and follow him
back
through the single lens
of his rifle

Winter Term

we are all seven
and wash our hands
of mothers
line up for high tea
hold out palms
reverse them for inspection
    fidget our fingers
on the backs of chairs
our mouths
ask for grace
to make us truly thankful

upstairs in Matron's sitting room
the gas fire exhales
a honeycomb of heat
dressing-gowned
we glean
fringes of its breath
line up for milk
of magnesia
halibut liver oil
and hot water for bottles
        she examines our tongues for signs
of constipation
paints our throats with iodine
and twirls cotton wool
round a wooden matchstick

Jenny covers her ears
screams
when Matron grips her single blonde braid
the matchstick
scours wax
from the slender
tube of her ear
        under our slippers
uneven floorboards whimper

Guy Fawkes Night

every November the fifth
the bonfire flickered
masks over faces
hot and close
we chanted
until Guy flared
into shimmered air
flying ash

in the leaf-smoky night
we raked his red furnace
for crusty black potatoes
while shadows loped
over the playing field
and left fountains of silver rain
the pink brilliance of roman candles
        we covered our ears
for each delicious
bang and crack
breathed the curly gunpowder air
and when jumping jacks
snapped our heels
we ran
crazy as Catherine wheels
sizzling on the fence

we followed rockets
whooshing
into whatever was beyond
where space ended
watched green and gold stars
fall slowly as feathers
wink
and leave the sky black again

Surgical Consultation

my father said *don't*
mention the word

cut   lump   out
of your mouth
she must never unravel
her pain
never understand where
the thread
ends

my father hid
my mother's tumour
in the pearled egg of a blow fly
a lie
left to hatch
in the dark
meat of daughters

Swallowing My Mother

a child's throat won't open
for a lost name
any more than lips
for a spoon
of frog-spawn-sized tapioca
in the school's deserted
dining room

my tongue refused to force
those glutinous
opaque eyes
down my throat
I still can't
form her name
mummy
without my mouth remembering
the position the tongue takes
before tears

Hymns Ancient and Modern

there were four hundred and sixty-eight Sundays
in twelve years (accounting
of course for the holidays)
Sunday at school
was an extra hour in bed
white blouses
(mended on Saturday)
black shoes polished four hundred and sixty-eight times
and hats
with throat-tight elastic

Sunday was boiled eggs
in the dining room with thirty-seven tables
and smashing a hole
in the keel of empty egg shells
so witches
couldn't use them for boats
      when a spoon rang a glass
we stilled it with a finger on the rim
to stop a sailor drowning
O Lord of Hosts we sing to Thee
For those in peril on the sea
if I'd had a voice
I'd have sung the ships home on Sundays
the rising notes like wind in the mast
the long slow sweep of music
taking me to the crest and down
into the belly of the wave

Sunday was two by two
up the empty high street
with the Book of Common Prayer
Hymns A & M
a penny for the collection
and bells tumbling over themselves
because it was eleven o'clock everywhere
    I prayed until hassocks
itched my knees
watched sun rays
angle through emerald glass
(on which the Lamb of God grazed)
slide down dusty chutes
and turn my hands green

I hungered
for a tuneful tongue
when incense of asters and roots
rose into a forest
of stone columns
Come ye thankful people come
Raise the song of Harvest-home
wheat sheaves leaned
on a pulpit darkened with centuries of sermons
the nave's neck filled with cabbages
loaves of bread
and green-striped vegetable marrows
big as piglets and ringing with ripeness
We plough the fields and scatter
The good seed on the land
my lips moved
but I only sang in my head

when we came to a *competent age*
and the vicar catechised
on Sunday afternoons
the odour of God lay dank as bones
please   I begged
by the canopied tomb in the transept
        marble Sir Thomas
        his wife and two children (taken in infancy)
let me be able to sing
but communion wafers
stuck to my tongue
I studied the Table of Kindred and Affinity
learned whom a woman may not marry
and every month
I bled
the curse indeed
all through Sunday evening bible class
and lantern slides of the Holy Land
I sat on my hands
afraid
I'd bloodied the back of my skirt

Sundays in December
when silver descants decorated carols
I watched the choir
walk two by two up the high street
past the war memorial
where poppy wreaths still
stained the granite red
past shops
whose paper garlands
and fold-out green bells peeked
from blind Sunday windows
I crossed my fingers
said I didn't mind
that I couldn't
sing

Every Child Must be Outside at Playtime

the common room is empty except
for Judy tucked
above the summer-cold radiator
blue striped cotton dress
crook'd knees
Clarke's sandals
brace her window nook

she knows camouflage
means don't move
become your surroundings
one of the wooden
foot-square lockers
where she doesn't keep
a drawstring bag of jacks
skipping rope   Pickup Sticks
anything that takes two
to play

outside
the tennis ball talks
against brick wall
hot asphalt
she
can't play here
can't play here
girls scramble in the sunny cleft
of cloakroom and common room walls

Judy is still reading
Swallows and Amazons   Frenchman's Inn
The Cruel Sea
the strawberry
pink birthmark
smeared
down the room-side
of her face

Legacy

(Aunt Lucy's version)

your great-grandmother reigned
sailed with Mama
and Papa on their honeymoon
voyage to a new African home
returned to England five years later
with widowed Mama
us three

your great-grandmother spent years in bed
her long dying upstairs
where photographs
of us   her grandchildren
stood like targets
on the dresser
our pocket handkerchiefs
bait
in the drawer below

each day we attended
Grandmama's morning ritual
kissed her
opened the drawer
found bad children's photographs
banished
to this bed of linen

your uncle and I
spent weeks face down   unrepentant
but your father
always upright
first born upon the dresser
never learned to laugh
like we do

Letters from Colonial West Africa

my dearest wife

every week
every year
his fountain pen graced
a white savannah of paper
line and loop elegant as gazelles
told the day's trek
quinine and fever
a date for a long promised leave

his brush caught bushbuck
mid-stride
a kob's muzzle
lifted from the river
the hartebeest's long face

until

his feet faltered
hands stammered
cramped words drooped
down the page
his pencil quavered
animals empty
as carcasses on market stalls

he came home
a shaven Samson
wore tweeds
fumbled buttons
and when his daughter did not kiss him
he wept

Paralysis Agitans

when Dr. Parkinson described the shaking palsy
he never noted how tremors
widened cracks
between father and daughter

I had to pretend
they were invisible
but the evidence
fell off his fork every evening
shirt buttons became too intricate
for his hands
kisses
scratchy reefs of stubble
white linen handkerchiefs soaked
with drool

those last teenage summers
of gasoline and cut grass
I watched him stumble
behind the mower
wished I looked like
someone else's daughter
that my father stood tall
and only the world
shook

For Sale: Number 47 Pandale Road

lightly used by ex-colonial his mother two children
and second wife
a detached yellow brick Victorian house
large drawing room (accommodates grand piano)
dining room   walled garden with mulberry tree
pears   apples   air raid shelter

here he hung the hallway with trophy skulls
empty sockets   decorated once a year with holly
black horns of bushcow
antelope and eland snuffing warmth
from the single paraffin heater
a black dot on the parquet floor below

here my father   tumbled hunter
eldest son
boast of my widowed grandmother
locked and bolted the front door
every night at ten

here the shaking palsy ambushed
his lively land of movement
the dark continent of his brain
set snares for his hands
stalked his feet
not with quick finger and recoil
but slow net and pit

here my grandmother practised
the art of concealment
plastered brown paper covers
around *Coping with Chronic Illness*
scissored medical reports from the paper
buried her widowed son's disease
behind her eyes
pronounced tremor   blank face
invisible

here the secret made dinner indigestible
children turned sour
furtive as leopards
their eyes drank brown soup
from flat rimmed bowls

here the tangling mesh descended
slowly as silk
twig by broken twig

here his neck stiffened
thigh staggered
hooves trembled
saliva drooled from his thick blue tongue

here in the pit
of his family

Man at Window

(Oil on canvas)

the man who stands with his back to us in the shadow of the second floor French window has come upstairs to watch his daughter walk to the taxi stand at the far end of the road

he has trapped his hands in the pockets of his dark suit concealed the tremor that agitates his fingers against the pads of his thumbs confirmed the linen folds of a handkerchief he will press to the corner of his mouth the moment after our glance shifts

his daughter steps out of the unseen scrap of urban garden the hawthorn's filigree shade into the sharp lemon light of the empty street   he has warned her that life is not a game warned against taking a job without a pension that every woman should cook well to be circumspect when riding in a third class carriage warned that the middle-aged man next door paints nudes never to set her purse down on a park bench but still she walks away leaving an oval steamship label on the polished half-moon table under the hall mirror

the balcony's stone balustrade separates him from the suggestion of early leaves along the tree-lined road an ochre row of three-story Victorian houses with blank glass eyes the sidewalk's long perspective a tiny black cab waiting at the vanishing point everything static except his daughter
now a brushstroke of Prussian blue

if she had understood what he meant to say she would have stayed to watch the single hawthorn in the pocket garden below flower again one branch alizarin crimson the other flake white a shared astonishment of blossom

Open House

this is the dining room   dark
lace curtains thick
with smog
mahogany table set
with bowls of Windsor soup
my father dishing up the penalty for not
talking to our new
stepmother

this the kitchen confessional
where my sister and I
washed secrets
the speciality of the house
never spoke of
our dead   talked
all through the nine o'clock radio news
then tuned in Saturday's
Forces Favourites
listened to lovelorn
messages for British soldiers
on the Rhine

we never thought of going *to*
only *away*
finding a place to fit
regular as teeth
rooted in the mother gums
smiling and white
never a hint of decay
bad blood
between us

The Brown Leather Suitcase

packed with numbered envelopes
my mother's
accounting for letters
sometimes lost
to censor or torpedoed ship
her four blue pages
unfold onto a thriving garden and children
day-old chicks
settled in her hand-built wooden and wire mesh run
a good crop of beans *at least*
the children are well nourished
you should see them play
rough and tumble with the dog

the still dark ink
her round hand
take charge of the page
the kitchen boiler
stayed alight until morning
last night waves of our bombers
droned overhead for two hours
your mother writes
she's practising first aid
at the Air Raid Post and never
sounded more lively

the hens grow large and lay
I brought your Aunt Edith two fresh eggs
for her birthday
she'll be the envy
of all her neighbours
we cycled five miles to her house
Tessa on her small bike
Julie in the carrier on mine

silence extends into months
do you still get my letters?
I write every week
your daughter asks 'is that Daddy'
and kisses the picture
on my dressing table
    Mrs. Johnson who helped
when Tessa had scarlet fever
must report for war work
the weeds are getting the better
of me

    letters received and kept
    for years
I would like to take the children
to visit Ellen in the country
you remember she's Julie's godmother?
but no unnecessary travel is allowed
the war
can't last for ever
our baby
starts school next month
I'm sorry
you've missed all
their growing up

P.S.   they're both keen to know names
of plants and butterflies
sometimes it seems I've forgotten
everything
I once knew   love,

White Dwarf   Still Emitting Light

I have a nebulous
wish for two and one-half
children   an English
timbered house called *The Goslings*
or *Fountain Cottage*
an orchard   two cats   one dog
and enough grazing for a child's pony

but nothing quite fits
I'd miss my suburban garden
the cluster
of alley and street
    the wish feels alien
uncomfortably rich
for a childless woman from a prairie city
like ordering too much coffee and baklava
or wearing your mother's fur coat

that's it
I'm in the wrong constellation
this
belongs to my mother
her metal bed
armoured with glossy pages of *Country Life*
prospects of freehold property denying
her colon harbours a tumour
her belly's density
the white room   ether
and methylated spirits
her daughters
a Gemini shimmer on the bed's horizon
the stillborn son
quickening again inside her womb

2:00 am

my hands still smell of bristlecone pine
the odour   a piece without a puzzle

I dream of avalanches   they fall
red   silent   ripe as raspberries

my mother was a river   I forget
the taste of fresh water

I learned how to be a woman
from the public library

the lump I finger through my night-dress
leaves my hands mute

in the house that smelled of polished wood
my grandmother sewed her own shroud

Spare Room

apples lie on the narrow bed
fill the room with ripeness
leaves of lemon verbena
hang in bunches
lavender spills
dried blossom on spread newspaper
   Granny still calls it
Moira's room
but no one sleeps
where locked windows
look over the cherry tree
and the ocean caught
in the hills' notch

      sea mist muffles the garden
      blankets bamboo
      drips from fretted edges
      of the cherry's last leaves
      drenches a spider's web hung
      on the glass pane
      comforts the cobbled yard below
      embraces a child
      leaning from the window
      falling into fog

Next of Kin: The Garden

agapanthus   the blue lily
cool as the virgin
pungent eucalyptus
grown from seed by my grandfather
heather and carpets of bees
curtains of fuchsia
red hot pokers
burning the border

orange nasturtiums and I run wild
where yellow iris
margins the pond's lush mud
peacock and tortoiseshell wings shiver
amethyst blooms
in the butterfly bush

never content to stay outside
the garden climbs to the bathroom window
moth-white jasmine
layers the air with nectar
all night
I lie in sheets that dried on lavender hedges
in licking waves
of long grass
the garden's arms

Turning Back the Sheets

after the children have gone
and dusk settles
on urban poplars
like hens settle on straw
I open the kitchen door
and call my grandmother back
from memory
from the garden
from where she once called me

she has gathered the hens into their house
left them idly
questioning their eggs
in the early dark
    hunched over the garden fork
(taken to parry the slash
of the rooster's claws)
she walks back
between rows of vegetables
    digs a dandelion's ivory root
from the dark mouth
of soil
    tells herself
tomorrow
I must pick gooseberries

this evening
at her walnut desk in the drawing room
she will write: *dear child*
after you left
I went to change the bed
but the sheets were warm
and still held
the smell of your body in their arms

Request Stop

excuse me   my aunt taps
the foreman's elbow
he settles his hard hat
back on his head and looks down
this tree
(her cane points to the evergreen
the line crew attack)
is a deodar
sacred
in the Himalayas

my father had a passion for travel
Nepal
and the Sea of Marmara
while I wait for the bus
I often think of the old country
and the trees
that made his garden
our geography
eucalyptus   *yucca*   *white pine*
and the deodar's blue skirts
where we children waited
in cedar dark
for stealthy paws of snow leopards

stroke the needles   she says
when the chain saw chokes
aren't they lush
as eyelashes?
Cedra deodara   (she flags the bus
with her shopping bag)
even the name feels delicious
in my mouth

careful boys
says the foreman
as my aunt climbs into the bus
one step
at a time
this here tree's
a deodar

Left Bank Reprise

in a Philadelphia hospital
the nun from Prague
leans over the white sheets
her wooden crucifix swinging
below the pink stethoscope
listens
to a winged heart
batter itself against a cage of ribs

are you Catholic?
she asks   nesting her hands
in her habit
my Irish aunt turns
in the rectangular bed
that is barely disturbed by her body
no   but before the war
I learned the Hail Mary in Paris

je Vous salue Marie   pleine de grace
their paired words glide
into the dark
ward   swallows
dipping to the evening
waters of the Seine

Ceremony

I bury the cat
under trees
among self-sown
Iceland poppies and blue columbines
I dig down to the frost line
a ritual unpliable
as rigor mortis
his old body
cranked to fit cardboard
winter boot box
his lips retracted   still
smelling the metallic taste of death
fur furrowed by the first
shovel of dirt
black   marmalade   tabby
it's a pattern
I follow
a memory of absence
filling in
for kindred and affinity
the dead
I've never attended
mother   father   grandmothers
favourite aunt
her daughter   the uncles
my mother's invincible sister
each spadeful
an old country funeral

Disconnection

the woman at the Y
shrugs receiver to mouth
while she hunts for my membership card
   I told him   she says to the phone
   'my dad works in Appliances'
   that you know
   all about fridges
she kisses   *bye*
love ya daddy
and cradles the phone
but she still can't find my card
I wonder if my lost

membership   daughtership
lies with my father's letters
that fretted
   why don't you bring your friends
   get a job closer
   to home
paper that trembled
   the least you can do
   is consult me
the love and kisses
absent   the space
a white bruise above his
formal closure

Bomb

I have not tasted
that name in my mouth
for so long
I am jealous
of a young woman soldier
pinned
in army bus wreckage

like white winged storks
sheets unfurl
and roost on the street
blood
weeps her face
her friends' flesh decorates
her dark hair

open eyed
among twisted metal ribs
dismembered arms
she calls
mummy   mummy help me I can't see

she names a luxury
mother
the word a cushion
on the hip of death

The House of Gemini

	in the house of Gemini
my sister and I are	Castor and Pollux
not twins we	live on different planes
hesitate to be close	optical siblings only
our relationship frail	a chance alignment
random as flotsam	on galactic seas
to pull ourselves nearer	we night watch
the same sky	the Big Dipper *called*
on different continents	*the Plough*
we match constellations	at spring's zenith
our binoculars split	a double star in the handle's crook
we mirror gesture inflection	Mizar & Alcor horse & rider
even neighbours mistake us	thirty light years apart
when I come home	

A Glossary of Green

Double Exposure

when winter snatched
breath from our mouths
hung it to dry
sharp white
on eyelashes
and fur trimmed hoods

you shelled yourself
inside your parka cowl
shared kernel
with flurries of chickadees
their scrupulous feet
perched on your bare
hand
a fist transformed
into a delicacy
of fingers

Winter Rules

Graffiti on Centre Street Bridge

the prairie is chastened
and white
but winter still
demands genuflection
on the sidewalk
compliance
when he freezes conversation
forces *weather permitting*
from our mouths

his ivory molars fracture light
make the lake moan
his tongue slicks
eighteen wheelers into the ditch
the highway black
ice conjured
from early morning air

winter's lips kiss
cold metal
fill the downspout's throat
with thirsty clumps of promise
rarely reveal
reasons for his night visit to the river bridge
   the cardboard bedrooms
   morsels of heat
   he draws from bony fingers
   his night-time necrophilia

Snow Eater

this mountain lion
devours a thousand skyfuls
of snow
    her sweet lush mouths
hunt down western slopes
drink the spruce trees' mounded boughs down to the green
gulp bowls of snow from the foothills
bite fat drifts in roadside ditches
suck the white stubble dry
    her hot tongues
never satisfied
until they lick the brown plate
of prairie
clean

Tri-Fruit Marmalade

pad the house with February fog
banish sidewalk and fence
shut off the hoar frost fountain
the silver birch in mid-spill
fill the kitchen with gusts of oranges
and occasional light lemons

paint your table a still life
with white plates
pock-skinned oranges
lemons with Cyrano noses
a buxom grapefruit
cut and careless
of its pink compartments
fleshy thighs

don't listen to the flamenco flavour
the bitter-sweet oranges from Seville
that toss the love
of lemons away
with a flick of their brilliant skirts
dice that haughty peel
rat-a-tat pits into a pectin cup
let the golden fruit simmer
dance
the fandango together

on foggy days
make marmalade with your lover
until your hands are sticky
with desire and spilled juice

Easter Long Weekend

all down the sun-warm street
garage doors rumble and squeak
we lean on garden rakes
relearn names
of neighbour children
who spent all winter concealed
in parka cocoons

the girls
(who last fall
trundled tricycles down our driveway)
emerge dragonfly bright
and swoop
on pink two wheelers
their brother
(hatched from a bunting bag)
squats on remnant ice
gutter water bubbling
over neon yellow boots

Variegations on Green

Sir James Walker Creek

this mountain pocket
is full of green
lake   spruce   meadow rue   valerian
mille feuille
which blossoms white
into yarrow
white   the umbelliferous
parasols of cow-parsnip
      lichen   larch   *Aquilegia*
yellow
goatsbeard and the globe
of its perfect clock that keeps
green on the move
aster   *Epilobium*
re-name themselves purple
magenta
the green can't stop
translating
even lake changes
to creek
tumbles white

C-Level Cirque

five fathoms
beneath the wind's rush
the pine-needled path muffles boots
flows upstream
through lean trunks
black ripples
of lodge poles

our limbs
    sunk in the green pine deeps
unlearn their locomotion
we swim through leafy shallows of arnica
shoals of bone-white bunchberry
stroke past
floating clematis
the orchid pink pearls
of Venus' slippers tucked
beneath the jade waters of underbrush
until slicker-yellow bells
of glacier lilies predict a border
an interface of elements

our boots strike rock
break the surface
of undulating trees
we breathe
the buoyancy of air
fly the bright snow view
of lake and sky

Writing Above Timberline

above eight thousand feet
the energy of emptiness
pushes back larch
lifts up
stone valleys

alpine tundra
rejects formal script
it splashes lichen graffiti
orange   yellow   grey/green
on rock
cut to the core
by snow   wind
    the wildness
of an open page

Clearing

Sawmill site (1896 - 1915) with barn and foreman's house

nothing true   only roofless
sway-backed lumber   does this house
listen to its fallen walls?

again magenta
fireweed quilts the bent iron
head and frame of a double bed

what did the foreman
believe when he planted blue
lilacs outside the front door?

baked potatoes cried
in the oven   sparrows
made windowsill love and war.

wood keeps lingering
memories in the grain
when will sky be sufficient roof?

rotting boards nurse trees
the clearing promises spruce
and a healing of old wounds

Cult/ivation

making the wild suitable for crops

the garden covets
this woman who works him
with naked hands
his children glisten
cheek by cheek
ruby and pickle green in her earthen cellar
       together they make vegetables fruitful
raspberries and rhubarb
zucchini   spaghetti squash   an abundance
of wax beans

when frost flays
the garden's green coat
she pulls netted gems
garnet beets from his deep pockets
he begs her   *keep kneeling*
next year I'll give you immaculate asparagus
six foot screens of corn

the garden   hard
under his white surplice
of snow
endures the parsnips' brass spikes
abides by the rule
of silence in winter
prostrate in the dark
galleries   cold cloisters
he visions Jerusalem artichokes
their knobbed tubers
nuzzling his palms
waits for the woman
to turn him over
in spring

Tomato: (Lycopersicon esculentum)

from tomatl, a fruit once prized by the Aztec

she was nine when Mr. Evans caught her
playing on his five-barred
garden gate
boys' voices and a referee's whistle
flowed water clear
from the parish playing grounds
while she kicked her sandals
on dusty wheel ruts
and swung the field gate
open again

she was afraid
he'd block the lane
with his pig-sty boots
torn jacket belted with twine
but he gave her one scarlet tomato
watched her lip
the sheened and sun-hot skin
nibble an entry
suck out pulp and seed

she never knew
when he lifted
the hem of her cotton skirt
those plump round fruits
had other names
wolf's peach
pomme d'amour
tomatl
eaten in ritual
exchange at night
seed
dripping down lips

Earth Tongues

English is the only language
to distinguish mushrooms
from toadstools
it fears
these doubtful plants
   cadaver pale
   or painted like city whores
life that lurks in woods
and needs no light

English gathers mushrooms
from the home field
but never eats in fairy rings
knows toadstools
inflame the flesh
make dead wood bloom and glow at night
that fungal names fill shelves
in witches' larders
   dead-man's fingers   jelly hedgehog
   poison pie

other lips
consume the cornucopia blossoming in darkness
   trompettes de la mort   chantarelles
   dead trees ripe with honey fungus
they devour devil's eggs
before these stinkhorns hatch
and thrust
under the rhododendron's skirts
all night

Sentinel Pass, September 25

this view
      Wenkchemna Glacier
      ten cloudless peaks across the valley
holds my gaze
while the trail to snow line
consumes your figure

wait

I am not ready
for the coming fast
of short days
I'm hungry still for green
delicious because it is our last
meal of the season

my eyes
ravenous as caterpillars
stuff themselves with kinnikinnick
juniper   mountain avens
snow willow
      every blink
must fill my larder
provide for seven long monochrome months

the ochre avalanche slopes
still leak grass
let me pull a stem
drink its glossary of green
before we reach the abstinence
of winter
the mourning
of snow

Dust

dust
composed
of the smallest
particles
the mite's
excreta
molecules from the cretaceous
lake bed's rim
thrust up
eroded
       one white hair
from a black cat's belly
spores from yesterday's
fungal ripening
five scales from a miller moth's wing
afloat on the curtain's
flurry
our own skin
cells
in atmospheric
premonition
of what we shall become
scintillating
under the sun's
long yellow
fingernail

Functional Anatomy

muscle   fascia   palm   life line
twenty-seven bones in each hand
a phalanx of four
fingers oppose the thumb
digits count
make a steeple
handle an axe
hear the heart
bleed
bind flesh to the bone

carry warm water
stainless
steel bowl to the bedside
uncurl fists
wash away the stink of dead
white skin
dry
hands no longer in touch
hands that tie
knots in blankets
lace themselves together
until tendons are strings
that forget how
to lie still

Storm

in a cold fever
of rain
thunder tumbling
the long bones of night
you get up

leave your man still
sleeping   stretched
out   arm flung beside your pillow
he is fasting and
too vulnerable to love
you watch

the crab apple's black
leafed branches shudder
in amber rain
falling
straight as cedar pencils
all night
you have dreamed of blood

and green gowns
catheter bags full
as udders and cloudy
with infection
ligaments of lightning
tart and appleflesh white
galvanize the neighbour's gutters
ache your teeth
you sit   blanket wrapped

in the kitchen waiting
for the pallid night
sky to change
at last the sun fingers
a space in the blue spruce
and gloss drips
down veins and midribs
of empty leaves
you know the stillness

wakes the man
his arm needled
and weary from hunting
the night
an empty bed
your body

Ruby Wedding Anniversary

Calgary Stampede

how long
asks the young woman at the gates
when we put down money
for one adult
one free senior's pass
how long have you been putting up with this fella?
forty years I say
                 and she slides back the bills
waves us both through
into a clamour of fried onions   Dodge'em cars
Country and Western

we hunt the sweet hay-sweat
of Percherons   dappled and black
proud feet of fetlocked Shires
shone brass and leather harnesses
the tambourines
of four horse teams
spinning their rigs
under the Big Top
        then scramble
from packed bleachers
(never say *careful*
are you sure it's safe?)
he jumps from the metal scaffold
I watch him drop
stumble
on a cardboard box
lurch backward
two inch bolt
slices
scalp
wound flows

into a bystander's pack of tissues
my hand
sticky and scarlet
his shirt soaked
blood
dropping on straw and the upturned brim
of my new white
cowboy hat

Night Shift

after midnight
the heart drops into a cold flow
a rift of small hours
where blood thins
and the last breath
sighs from a chest

renewal or death
we are bound
by the same biology
as plants

in the rich humus of night
the cycle begins
again   one grows from another
heads bud
limbs extend like leaves
lungs fill with the first breath of green light
mouths rooting
for the dark nipple
of earth

Apnea

the snowless
night consumes your shape
in the bed beside me
your regular breath
shallows
and slips between palate and tongue
disappears
down the slimmest of burrows
emerges

a ghost expiration

I count seconds
get up on my elbow
test the motionless air at your mouth
hunt the flat of your chest
with fingers
nocturnal as whiskers
searching
for an underground
tremor of heart
the absent lift of ribs

then your jaw jerks
a long deep gasp
fills lungs
like rain driving
snow into April black earth
a renewal
that leaves us
easy prey
for the omnivorous night

Cold Comfort

coke in cans   cold beef   avocados
their reptilian skin
bruised purple
coffee from Costa Rica
kept for best but never used
potatoes sprouting for spring
frail white arms pleading for burial
in the frozen garden
and cheese
    white Brie
    creamy hearted Camembert
    Emmenthaler   its vacant spaces
    hardened into hemispheres
    pumpkin coloured rat trap cheese
    bright and sharp as a guillotine
    and processed cheese packaged
    in neat foil shrouds

below the butter keeper
the red lidded jar
an emergency preserve
of numbers and notes
insurance company
funeral plans
instructions for lost cats
and what to do when the furnace goes out

Roving Doesn't Mean
We'll Never Come Home

I'm going down town again

where will you park?
I tell you
       on a well lit street
don't tell you
I like
feral cats that scavenge
a pawn shop shadow
the alley's
piss and beer breath
emergency sirens
agitating
a rumble
of cars
doors that spear
the sidewalk with light
purge
a babble of voices
close again
I like the strident
night signs
red and green
mirrored
in wet black streets
the lemony taste
of risk

Springing Loose

the black cat crouches
at the base of the fence
he's bony
an inveterate wanderer
rescued from his last
day at the pound
it's easy to fence him in
   he's thirteen
no longer able
to alight with grace on a fence rail
or prowl an apple tree
he must glimpse
the glories of the back alley
through hexagons of wire

I pace the corner of winter
hungry for Greece
the Galápagos and Great Slave Lake
   this urgency fills us both
we long to be lost
crave the bite
of nights without houses
an orchestra
of grass
a ticket with no
destination

    on this last night of winter
    we lie within house walls
    listen
    ears pricked
    chin on paws
    to the earth in estrous

rain fondles the window
a bark ricochets
inside night's hollow chambers
roots shimmy through soil
box cars clatter down tracks
cut loose
from the string

roving doesn't mean we'll never come home
we don't wander long
four hours
or three weeks
and we're back curled
in the corner of the couch
with tales of mice
or Venice

Detour

I love travel
stores that offer
bags and pouches
with multiple pockets
for escudos or drachmas
shelves that hold the hundred
churches of Quito
a white washed Aegean
the spice coloured odour of India
books that imply
obligation
Lonely Planet

Closing the Book in the Semi-Tropical Forest

our own words
shiver winter between us
we read this anthology of palms
one by one
butterfly   fan   date
fill our last chapter
with bird of paradise   edible fig
banana's banner leaves
the moist peat-mossed earth
a conflagration of green
lit by the dense white scent
of lemon blossom
the Superb Starling's
metallic flash

crop full of grain and sliced tropical fruit
the bird preens in the crowns
of galvanized struts
roosts in risen heat
caught
by the glass hull
that separates us
our green fiction
from winter's white
truth

Continental Drift

We say that the firmament is full of stars, as though it
were equally full; but we know that there are more stars
under the Northern than under the Southern Pole.
      John Donne   *from Meditation XIII*

go north with me
take a bearing from Polaris
and we'll walk where spruce refuse to root
    tell no one where we are
or where we might set foot
teach me language
    snow stinging
or vole's pink voice below
the prairie fescue
singing
    bring me rumors
from a peat-dark wind
tales of berry bogs on fire with frost

       jump ship with me
       when southern cross
       floats high on outer reef
          I'll show you soundless language
       luminescent lips
       of giant clams
       violet parrot fish that mouth
       the coral walls
          we'll swim together
       weightless
       in these underwater clefts
       I'll teach you languid finning
       bubbled breath

dive the reef with me
this single night a year
when full moon
conjugates with coral
spawns a milky way
where gametes fuse and drift
on tidal whim
a cloud
of rising stars
your recompense
for northern
firmament
its distant shards of light

Slipping the Night's Moorings

a pyromaniac sun
torches clouds
blackens the hump
of Green Island
leaves eight-mile beach empty
except for my body
lying on sand
smoother than unslept sheets
in the Royal Mariner Hotel

jazz from the beachside diner boils
over the sidewalk
hot and syrup thick
cheap gardenia scent
and the steam of cooked crab
pump from open windows
      I hear your hands in the darkness
know they sound the sweat
the warm waters
of women

you dance your catch
high and tight
play her
when she plunges
desperate for deep water
you smell of blood
and silver scales
I won't
open my mouth

night roosts
plush and thick in the candled
frangipani trees
the tide puckers the sea's polyester sheen
its fingers foam and hush the shore
        snuff out
the wax pink blossoms
I am casting off
my dress
dancing with the sea

Balcony and Sea View

I love the reiteration of waves
showing me   showing me   showing me
the ocean's green mouth
the spume
of its salty breath

but the sea is so protective
pleading *hush   hush*
all night
as if the wind
that tosses the palm leaves like stallions' tails
might rush in and take me

the wind whistles in the rigging
ding-ding-dings its fingers on the masts
waits for me
to open the bedroom window
let it curl through the gap
belly the curtain
ruffle my hair

I love the wind
wanting me
to come outside and ride the palm tree stallions

Slip-Dreaming in the Glow-Worm Grotto

Waitomo, New Zealand

drop below
leaf gloss   tree tangle
          Waitomo: *water flows into a hole*
leaches limestone
leaves a honeycomb
of pothole   cave   echo
tack-hammer drip
builds albino
stalactite and stalagmite

water flows   the boat
drifts a mine-black
cavern dilates the eye
scatters it with constellations

glow-worm filaments
necklace roof and ledge
an arm's length
or a light year away
silence
transmutes the moist galaxy
old star-shapes appear
Great Bear   Sky Dog
a cluster
of ancient comforts
          a cave's dank smell
memory of fire
familiar patterns of night

Blooming Out Loud

Alpbach, Austria

every year geraniums start a revolution
against green
that carpets the valleys and alps

pink   vermilion
they crowd the whitewashed *Rathaus* windows
lean on their elbows and gossip
all day long

even at the most demure *Pension*
they cascade over balconies
late at night
tumble over the carved hearts
make bawdy jokes
about long johns and bloomers
drying under the eaves

geraniums will never grow up

when velvet cows sway
down the village street
rollicking blooms
spill from wooden watering troughs
and shout
here, drink!

the Brown Swiss cows lower their horns
roll their eyes and trot
bells swinging
into prim green pastures
leave the geraniums
sprawled around the pump
reckless and scarlet
with laughter

Michaelskapelle

Hallstat, Austria

beyond immaculate
headstones   red begonias   votive lamps
the chapel
houses a thicket of bones
sorted anatomically
femur tibia radius ulna
the skulls piled
lettered with name and life-span
painted with a cap of roses
    an ivy wreath
    nothing but a cross
earth-worn globes and frames
dredged from soil
too steep   too precious
for departed flesh
to occupy for long
   this charnel house displays
a redemption from the grave
the frugal necessity
of mountain
living

Village Talk

the black cat and I
lie in the garden hammock
while the cobalt throat of evening swallows
the last portion of light
we're taking bets
on a conjunction
of the full moon and Venus

    half a mile down the road the curate
    three parishioners and the organist
    sing evensong in the twelfth century
    square towered church
    Lord now lettest Thou Thy servant depart in peace
    the psalm leaks from stained glass
    windows and open door
    blends with crushed geranium leaves
    and creosote from the railway
    four fields away

the village says
    last week
    the publican's wife who wears
    red shoes and no stockings
    on her tanned and hairless legs
    left for good
Ma says
    her husband
    with his gypsy looks
    and that way with the women
    has snared
    the doctor's daughter
    behind the hedge
    their voices drift

    I dream prairie snow
fine white flakes
wind gusting flurries
into a street lamp's halo

when I wake
Venus ascends her southern path alone
the cat has caught the moon
in a lacy basket of leaves
his eyes
drink her light

The White Double Bed

the foghorn carries
a long vowel over the mainland
fretful waves jangle bell-buoys
the ocean's iron tongues
   the newly drowned
housed in the forms
of harbour seals
take a last look at shingle
grey shore

pull off your sea-boots Ryan Joseph
there's only water to fill them
your hair swings in a forest of brown kelp
and the foghorn is a silence
in my belly
your woollen jersey knits me cold
as goose flesh
its cables unravel
into my lap
the priest says   *when the lovely milk*
flows in your breast
and the young one sucks
you must forget
how he was conceived
remember
four walls   white sheets
the lovely hands of lust
that led us through ragweed and stone fields
remember feather beds of heather
remember when you fed me blackberries
we dowsed the hills with a hazel twig
and conjured water

now my mouth
is a long vowel
even a child
could walk through the dark
eyes of seals   into the domes
of their sleek grey heads

Place Of Birth

El Salvador

in English
as a second language
Maria reads the Christmas story
from a child's book   follows
the pregnant woman and the carpenter
weary from walking
     like I was
she says   her hand remembering
     a nine month belly

     Maria   married at fifteen
     works her own plot of land
     in a valley wealthy
     with corn   lemons   beans   melons

     when soldiers come
     her uncle   deaf since birth
     is gathering fruit in a leaf thick
     orange tree
       rifles raised
     they order him   *bájate*
     twice
      before picking
     him off

Maria's finger ploughs
across the page
comes up short against
stable
      a house for horses or cows
the tutor says
     women escape
     into chill mountains
     walk higher every day
     Maria's first son
     born   a night stop
     in a hillside donkey shelter
       the villagers
     harvested three times
     by soldiers and
     guerrillas
     want the women gone but give
     Maria a clean dress
     rags for the baby who will never
     follow her
     out of this
     country of their birth

Night Talk around the Casa Degli Olivi

Lago di Garda

thunder doubles the hills
around the Bay of Mermaids
rolls syllables
through gauze curtains that bird-wing
into the bed room

a gravel shuffle of chairs
below the balcony
Senora Parisi racks
empty bottles of Bardolino
gathers glasses
locks the iron garden gate

lightning ricochets
from mountain to lake
stilettos the dark
columnar cypress
sears ivory ribs
of lawn chairs
onto the eye

now   rain

     a declension
thick as Mediterranean hair
don't close the shutters
don't shut out
the Atlas cedar towering over the old palace wall
fill the mirror
with wet olive branches
invite the pungent limes
and dusky grapes that drink
in the vineyard above the house

adagio
linger over the vowel
the doubled consonant
bellissima
pleasure my tongue
listen to rain
talk on tiled roofs

Flowing to the Amazon

Rio Napo

beside the forest's milk-tea highway
roosters demand
dark disappear
from buttress root
and wet
hollow where frogs stroke
the shadow
of night's moist flavour
pack it away
in their treasury of mud

the forest is animate
and speaks
>   *dios te dé*
>   *god gives you*
toucans chant
from their dead snag
poised over thick ochre water
the fast canoe
with yesterday's machete wound
leaves
water slapping banks

>   downstream
>   a woman perfumed
>   with after-shave and sweat
>   riffles through a wad of bills
>   on the company's potholed
>   street behind the hospital

absence will soon fold over a face
and skin retreat
in deference to the scalpel
the forest gives
takes away

morning bleeds into the river's
gauze horizon

Athena's Cat

in the moon white street of steps
cat shapes   mute shadows
run belly to ground

under the fairy-lit plane tree
night is rich
with rosemary and grilled lamb
cheese dropping into hot oil
skillets scraping
bouzouki music
and the chatter of plates
fill the taverna's
green pool of light

her teats sucked dry
ear still oozing pus
the lean calico
magnifies her eyes   focuses
a hot spot on a cerebrum
draws hands
delectable with dolmades or calamari
under the tablecloth

she turns her head sidelong to chew
catches the waiter's black-trousered
leg ready to kick
and gathers her haunches
leaps so lightly
she might have flown
into green branches
that roof the restaurant

but before the retsina is gone
she's back by the tumbled columns
a pigeon clamped in her mouth
    behind her head
a winged shoulder unfurls
beats
the ancient air

Mirage

Kephalonia 1995

across from Hotel Eleni
a woman from a village of nightingales
pegs white undershirts
and tea towels
to her balcony line
she croons to a yellow flutter
of caged canaries

below her
the languid dock
empties   the Lixouri ferry dissolves
in a distant shimmer of waves
the seller of basil and marjoram
lies in the citrus shade
of his neighbours' stall
thinks of a woman he wants
quartering lemons
for the evening meal

a man drains a tepid bottle of Fanta
the girl in the fuchsia blouse
shrugs his arm from her shoulder
finds her face in the bakery window
lifts a sheet of hair
from the moist nape of her neck

next to the bus depot
hooked rabbits glisten
dressed
only in olive-sized eyes
and puff tails
the butcher dabs sweat
from his head
with a blood-smeared apron

> *when the air shivers and fills*
> *with the cold water song*
> *of nightingales*

> *the girl's hand*
> *closes her fuchsia collar*
> *rabbit haunches ripple*
>   *flesh remembering wild grass*
> *the herb seller gets to his feet*
> *chooses five lemons*

the canaries'
ruffled throats subside
the woman from the village of nightingales
shades the cage
with a moist towel

Reprisal

Trail above Mega Spileo Monastery, Greece
December 8 1943/ May 29, 1995

climbing beyond cliff and nested monastery
my boots follow
old footprints
perhaps
at this same turn in the path
brush snagged black robes
pulled them back to ikon and altar
here
the soldier's rifle
jabbed them onward

single file
is all the trail
allows
shuffled dust
bruised basil and thyme
musk of goat in the nostrils

the tremulous river is silent
stifled by height
boots stumble
knock a stone from the path
    the heart beats
the heart
beats the drum of the ear
steals blood
from muscle and skin
  clack of rock on rock
the stone strikes
drops
diminished
a patter of pebbles

         scatter
toward the ravine

monks and laymen
    bowels loosening
    at the tannic smell of steel
ascend
above cave and monastery
to this ledge of oregano
the air
so thick with prayer
surely it would bear bodies
gently through the dark matter
onto the floor
of the valley

their minds giddy
with invocation
with the mothers of sorrow
in the village
the men fall at last
tattered
with bullets
arms flung to clutch
the hands of saints reaching
from the opened lids of silver reliquaries

sacks of blood and bone
their bodies plunge and turn
robes fly
like ravens playing
in the limestone up-drafts

the mountains are void
stars are splinters of bone
from the charcoal skull of heaven

Destination Unknown

the young man in the all-night restaurant
five minutes from Washington
National Airport
sets his brown suitcase on a table and unpacks
    a traveller with nothing
to distinguish him but astonishingly pale blue eyes
his intensity
as he sets out tumblers
knives   forks   framed photographs
as if he always travelled with the family silver

will the next thing he'll set
to the left of the fork
be a bomb
I regret choosing this alcove without an exit
comfort myself
he's only afraid
of germs on restaurant dishes
    but perhaps he's planning
his last breakfast
wants to depart
in style

I want to know his flight number
where he's headed
but leave
    a five dollar bill for an unfinished
cup of coffee   half a muffin
check out
airport   ticket counter
departure lounge
buckle my seat belt and listen
for announcements
                    this is the final call

Open Window

Below Mount Helmós, Greece

the dark deciphers itself
node by node
undresses the plane tree
in the village *plateía*
where owl
and nimble voice of a nightingale
decorate opaque hours
of sleep

deciduous night washes away
with tiny declensions of darkness
a warren of small sounds
plash of water
dog turning in his dry
weed bed
shutter folding back
footfall on stony path

the waxing line of light
licks the ridge of the Nereids
watermelon dawn
the still
eyeless day
is now belled with goats
their limber legs
slender hooves
tap tapping a nimbus of dust
into the clear mountain pastures

Postcard View - Other Side Of Gulf

amber rock burnishes the morning
squeezes the harbour in bony arms
herds houses to the brink
of the cerulean sea
where men wash decks
shovel ice
feed the truck's dark belly
with shimmer of fish

across the street
men clatter window shutters
tuck in shirts
   I haven't yet eaten breakfast
but the café serves only coffee
to men
whose boats throbbed into port
at half past four this morning

I buy a hot *tirópita* at the bakery
join women at the bus station
         kaliméra I say
stack my back pack   sun hat   bottled water
with string-tied cardboard boxes
and shopping bags
   women in dark dresses
going to market for tomatoes   greens   more oil
ask if I'm on my own
         where I'm going
I can't speak Greek
but reply *Astakós*   (did the accent fall where it should?)
to the isthmus then Náfplio
the other side of the gulf
         bráva bráva they smile
beckon me into the shade
make sure I get on
when the bus arrives

gears whine and crawl
the bare brown hill
      kaló taxídi we wish through the window
      good journey
this one and beyond

Forty years ago Catherine Moss left England with the intention of travelling round the world. In Canada she worked in her chosen profession, occupational therapy, and planned a route to Australia. Then love intervened; she made a home – and a garden – in Alberta. From her parents and grandparents Moss inherited a delight in gardening and the desire for travel; over the last thirty-five years she and her husband have visited six continents. Her poetry has appeared in many Canadian literary magazines and has been broadcast on CBC radio. Moss edited FreeFall magazine for two years and taught poetry at the Alexandra Writers' Centre Society in Calgary.